THE SECOND 100 CHINESE CHARACTERS

TRADITIONAL CHARACTER EDITION

The Quick and Easy Method to Learn
the second 100 Basic Chinese Characters

Introduction by
Alison and Lawrence Matthews

TUTTLE PUBLISHING
Tokyo • Rutland, Vermont • Singapore

Published by Tuttle Publishing, an imprint of Periplus Editions (HK) Ltd, with editorial offices at 364 Innovation Drive, North Clarendon, Vermont 05759 and 130 Joo Seng Road, #06-01, Singapore 368357.

ISBN-10: 0-8048-3833-X
ISBN-13: 978-0-8048-3833-7

Distributed by:

Japan
Tuttle Publishing
Yaekari Building 3F
5-4-12 Osaki, Shinagawa-ku
Tokyo 141-0032, Japan
Tel: (03) 5437 0171
Fax: (03) 5437 0755
Email: tuttle-sales@gol.com

North America, Latin America & Europe
Tuttle Publishing
364 Innovation Drive
North Clarendon, VT 05759-9436
Tel: (802) 773 8930
Fax: (802) 773 6993
Email: info@tuttlepublishing.com
www.tuttlepublishing.com

Asia-Pacific
Berkeley Books Pte Ltd
130 Joo Seng Road, 06-01/03
Singapore 368357
Tel: (65) 6280 1330
Fax: (65) 6280 6290
Email: inquiries@periplus.com.sg
www.periplus.com

Indonesia
PT Java Books Indonesia
Kawasan Industri Pulogadung
Jl. Rawa Gelam IV No. 9
Jakarta 13930, Indonesia
Telp. (021) 4682 1088
Fax. (021) 461 0207
Email: cs@javabooks.co.id

09 08 07 06
8 7 6 5 4 3 2 1

Printed in Singapore

Contents

Introduction

Learning the characters is one of the most fascinating and fun parts of learning Chinese, and people are often surprised by how much they enjoy being able to recognize them and to write them. Added to that, *writing* the characters is also the best way of *learning* them. This book shows you how to write the second 100 most common characters and gives you plenty of space to practice writing them. When you do this, you'll be learning a writing system which is one of the oldest in the world and is now used by more than a billion people around the globe every day.

In this introduction we'll talk about:
- how the characters developed;
- the difference between traditional and simplified forms of the characters;
- what the "radicals" are and why they're useful;
- how to count the writing strokes used to form each character;
- how to look up the characters in a dictionary;
- how words are created by joining two characters together; and, most importantly;
- how to write the characters!

Also, in case you're using this book on your own without a teacher, we'll tell you how to get the most out of using it.

Chinese characters are not nearly as strange and complicated as people seem to think. They're actually no more mysterious than musical notation, which most people can master in only a few months. So there's really nothing to be scared of or worried about: everyone can learn them—it just requires a bit of patience and perseverance. There are also some things which you may have heard about writing Chinese characters that aren't true. In particular, you don't need to use a special brush to write them (a ball-point pen is fine), and you don't need to be good at drawing (in fact you don't even need to have neat handwriting, although it helps!).

How many characters are there?
Thousands! You would probably need to know something like two thousand to be able to read Chinese newspapers and books, but you don't need anything like that number to read a menu, go shopping or read simple street signs and instructions. Just as you can get by in most countries knowing about a hundred words of the local language, so too you can get by in China quite well knowing a hundred common Chinese characters. And this would also be an excellent basis for learning to read and write Chinese.

How did the characters originally develop?
Chinese characters started out as pictures representing simple objects, and the first characters originally resembled the things they represented. For example:

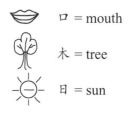

口 = mouth

木 = tree

日 = sun

Some other simple characters were pictures of "ideas":

一 one   二 two   三 three

Some of these characters kept this "pictographic" or "ideographic" quality about them, but others were gradually modified or abbreviated until many of them now look nothing like the original objects or ideas.

Then, as words were needed for things which weren't easy to draw, existing characters were "combined" to create new characters. For example, 女 (meaning "woman") combined with 子 (meaning "child") gives a new character 好 (which means "good" or "to be fond of").

Notice that when two characters are joined together like this to form a new character, they get squashed together and deformed slightly. This is so that the new, combined character will fit into the same size square or "box" as each of the original two characters. For example the character 日 "sun" becomes thinner when it is the left-hand part of the character 時 "time"; and it becomes shorter when it is the upper part of the character 星 "star". Some components got distorted and deformed even more than this in the combining process: for example when the character 人 "man" appears on the left-hand side of a complex character it gets compressed into 亻, like in the character 他 "he".

So you can see that some of the simpler characters often act as basic "building blocks" from which more complex characters are formed. This means that if you learn how to write these simple characters you'll also be learning how to write some complex ones too.

How are characters read and pronounced?

The pronunciations in this workbook refer to modern standard Chinese. This is the official language of China and is also known as "Mandarin" or "**putonghua**".

The pronunciation of Chinese characters is written out with letters of the alphabet using a romanization system called "Hanyu Pinyin"—or "**pinyin**" for short. This is the modern system used in China. In pinyin some of the letters have a different sound than in English—but if you are learning Chinese you'll already know this. We could give a description here of how to pronounce each sound, but it would take up a lot of space—and this workbook is about writing the characters, not pronouncing them! In any case, you really need to hear a teacher (or recording) pronounce the sounds out loud to get an accurate idea of what they sound like.

Each Chinese character is pronounced using only one syllable. However, in addition to the syllable, each character also has a particular *tone*, which refers to how the pitch of the voice is used. In standard Chinese there are four different tones, and in pinyin the tone is marked by placing an accent mark over the vowel as follows:

1st tone (high, flat) **mā**

2nd tone (rising) **má**

3rd tone (down-up) **mǎ**

4th tone (falling) **mà**

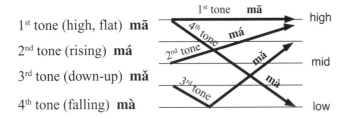

The pronunciation of each character is therefore a combination of a syllable and a tone. There are only a small number of available syllables in Chinese, and many characters therefore share the same syllable—in fact many characters share the same sound plus tone combination. They are like the English words "here" and "hear"—when they are spoken, you can only tell which is which from the context or by seeing the word in written form.

Apart from **putonghua** (modern standard Chinese), another well-known type of Chinese is Cantonese, which is spoken in southern China and in many Chinese communities around the world. In fact there are several dozen different Chinese languages, and the pronunciations of Chinese characters in these languages are all very different from each other. But the important thing to realize is that the characters themselves do *not* change. So two Chinese people who can't understand each other when they're talking together, can write to one another without any problem at all!

Simplified and traditional characters

As more and more characters were introduced over the years by combining existing characters, some of them became quite complicated. Writing them required many strokes which was time-consuming, and it became difficult to distinguish some of them, especially when the writing was small. So when writing the characters quickly in hand-written form, many people developed short-cuts and wrote them in a more simplified form. In the middle of the 20th century, the Chinese decided to create a standardised set of simplified characters to be used by everyone in China. This resulted in many of the more complicated characters being given simplified forms, making them much easier to learn and to write. Today in China, and also in Singapore, these simplified characters are used almost exclusively, and many Chinese no longer learn the old traditional forms. However the full traditional forms continue to be used in Taiwan and in overseas Chinese communities around the world.

Here are some examples of how some characters were simplified:

Traditional		Simplified
見	→	见
飯	→	饭
號	→	号
幾	→	几

Modern standard Chinese uses only simplified characters. But it is useful to be able to recognize the traditional forms as they are still used in many places outside China, and of course older books and inscriptions were also written using the traditional forms. This workbook teaches the full traditional forms. If there is a simplified form, then it is shown in a separate box on the right-hand side of the page so that you can see what it looks like.

How is Chinese written?

Chinese was traditionally written from top to bottom in columns beginning on the right-hand side of the page and working towards the left, like this:

幸福一點兒也不
難擁有。祇要妳
常為人着想，帶
來歡樂，妳會發
覺到那也是一種
幸福呀！

This means that for a book printed in this way, you start by opening it at (what Westerners would think of as) the back cover. While writing in columns is sometimes considered archaic, you will still find many books, especially novels and more serious works of history, printed in this way.

Nowadays, though, most Chinese people write from left to right in horizontal lines working from the top of a page to the bottom, just as we do in English.

Are Chinese characters the same as English words?

Although each character has a meaning, it's not really true that an individual character is equivalent to an English "word". Each character is actually only a single *syllable*. In Chinese (like in English) some words are just one syllable, but most words are made up of two or more syllables joined together. The vast majority of words in Chinese actually consist of two separate characters placed together in a pair. These multi-syllable words are often referred to as "compounds", and this workbook provides a list of common compounds for each character.

Some Chinese characters are one-syllable words on their own (like the English words "if" and "you"), while other characters are only ever used as one half of a word (like the English syllables "sen" and "tence"). Some characters do both: they're like the English "light" which is happy as a word on its own, but which also links up to form words like "headlight" or "lighthouse".

The Chinese write sentences by stringing characters together in a long line from left to right (or in a column from top to bottom), with equal-sized spaces between each character. If English were written this way—as individual syllables rather than as words that are joined together—it would mean all the syllables would be written separately with spaces in between them, something like this:

If you can un der stand this sen tence you can read Chi nese too.

So in theory, you can't see which characters are paired together to form words, but in practice, once you know a bit of Chinese, you can!

Punctuation was not traditionally used when writing Chinese, but today commas, periods (full stops), quotation marks, and exclamation points are all used along with other types of punctuation which have been borrowed from English.

Two ways of putting characters together

We have looked at *combining characters* together to make new *characters*, and *pairing characters* together to make *words*. So what's the difference?

Well, when two *simple characters* are combined to form a new *complex character*, they are squashed or distorted so that the new character fits into the same size square as the original characters. The meaning of the new character *may* be related to the meaning of its components, but it frequently appears to have no connection with them at all! The new complex character also has a new single-syllable pronunciation, which may or may not be related to the pronunciation of one of its parts. For example:

女		也		她
nǚ	+	**yě**	=	**tā**
woman		also		she
日		月		明
rì	+	**yuè**	=	**míng**
sun		moon/month		bright

On the other hand, when characters are *paired together* to create *words*, the characters are simply written one after the other, normal sized, with a normal space in between (and there are no hyphens or anything to show that these characters are working together as a pair). The resulting word has a pronunciation which is *two* syllables—it is simply the pronunciations of the two individual characters one after the other. Also, you're much more likely to be able to guess the meaning of the word from the meanings of the individual characters that make it up. For example:

大		人		大人
dà	+	**rén**	=	**dà rén**
big		person		adult
姐		妹		姐妹
jiě	+	**mèi**	=	**jiě mèi**
older sister		younger sister		sisters
四		月		四月
sì	+	**yuè**	=	**sì yuè**
four		moon/month		April
再		见		再见
zài	+	**jiàn**	=	**zài jiàn**
again		see; meet		Goodbye!

Is it necessary to learn words as well as characters?
As we've said, the meaning of a compound word is often related to the meanings of the individual characters. But this is not always the case, and sometimes the word takes on a new and very specific meaning. So to be able to read Chinese sentences and understand what they mean, it isn't enough just to learn individual character—you'll also need to learn words. (In fact, many individual characters have very little meaning at all by themselves, and only take on meanings when paired with other characters).

Here are some examples of common Chinese words where the meaning of the overall word is not what you might expect from the meanings of the individual characters:

明		天		明天
míng	+	**tiān**	=	**míng tiān**
bright		day/sky		tomorrow

好		在		好在
hǎo	+	**zài**	=	**hǎo zài**
good		be present at/ live at		fortunately

If you think about it, the same thing happens in English. If you know what "battle" and "ship" mean, you can probably guess what a "battleship" might be. But this wouldn't work with "championship"! Similarly, you'd be unlikely to guess the meaning of "honeymoon" if you only knew the words "honey" and "moon".

The good news is that learning compound words can help you to learn the characters. For example, you may know (from your Chinese lessons) that **xīng qī** means "week". So when you see that this word is written 星期, you will know that 星 is pronounced **xīng**, and 期 is pronounced **qī**—even when these characters are forming part of *other* words. In fact, you will find that you remember many characters as half of some familiar word.

When you see a word written in characters, you can also often see how the word came to mean what it does. For example, **xīng qī** is 星期 which literally means "star period". This will help you to remember both the word *and* the two individual characters.

What is a stroke count?
Each Chinese character is made up of a number of pen or brush strokes. Each individual stroke is the mark made by a pen or brush before lifting it off the paper to write the next stroke. Strokes come in various shapes and sizes—a stroke can be a straight line, a curve, a bent line, a line

with a hook, or a dot. There is a traditional and very specific way that every character should be written. The order and direction of the strokes are both important if the character is to have the correct appearance.

What counts as a stroke is determined by tradition and is not always obvious. For example, the small box that often appears as part of a character (like the one on page 94, in the character 口) counts as three strokes, not four! (This is because a single stroke is traditionally used to write the top and right-hand sides of the box).

All this may sound rather pedantic but it is well worth learning how to write the characters correctly and with the correct number of strokes. One reason is that knowing how to count the strokes correctly is useful for looking up characters in dictionaries, as you'll see later.

This book shows you how to write characters stroke by stroke, and once you get the feel of it you'll very quickly learn how to work out the stroke count of a character you haven't met before, and get it right!

What are radicals?
Although the earliest characters were simple drawings, most characters are complex with two or more parts. And you'll find that some simple characters appear over and over again as parts of many complex characters. Have a look at these five characters:

她 she
媽 mother
姐 older sister
好 good
姓 surname

All five of these characters have the same component on the left-hand side: 女, which means "woman". This component gives a clue to the meaning of the character, and is called the "radical". As you can see, most of these five characters have something to do with the idea of "woman", but as you can also see, it's not a totally reliable way of guessing the meaning of a character. (Meanings of characters are something you just have to learn, without much help from their component parts).

Unfortunately the radical isn't always on the left-hand side of a character. Sometimes it's on the right, or on the top, or on the bottom. Here are some examples:

Character	Radical	Position of radical
都	阝	right
星	日	top
您	心	bottom
這	辶	left and bottom

Because it's not always easy to tell what the radical is for a particular character, it's given explicitly in a separate box for each of the characters in this book. However, as you learn more and more characters, you'll find that you can often guess the radical just by looking at a character.

Why bother with radicals? Well, for hundreds of years Chinese dictionaries have used the radical component of each character as a way of indexing them. All characters, even the really simple ones, are assigned to one radical or another so that they can be placed within the index of a Chinese dictionary (see the next section).

Incidentally, when you take away the radical, what's left is often a clue to the *pronunciation* of the character (this remainder is called the "phonetic component"). For example, 嗎 and 媽 are formed by adding different radicals to the character 馬 "horse" which is pronounced **mǎ**. Now 嗎 is pronounced **ma** and 媽 is pronounced **mā**, so you can see that these two characters have inherited their pronunciations from the phonetic component 馬. Unfortunately these "phonetic components" aren't very dependable: for example 也 on its own is pronounced **yě** but 他 and 她 are both pronounced **tā**.

How do I find a character in an index or a dictionary?
This is a question lots of people ask, and the answer varies according to the type of dictionary you are using. Many dictionaries today are organized alphabetically by pronunciation. So if you want to look up a character in a dictionary and you know its pronunciation, then it's easy. It's when you don't know the pronunciation of a character that there's a problem, since there is no alphabetical order for characters like there is for English words.

If you don't know the pronunciation of a character, then you will need to use a radical index (which is why radicals are useful). To use this you have to know which part of the character is the radical, and you will also need to be able to count the number of strokes that make up the character. To look up 姓, for example, 女 is the radical (which has 3 strokes) and the remaining part 生 has 5 strokes. So first you find the radical 女 amongst the 3-stroke radicals in the radical index. Then, since there are lots of characters under 女, look for 姓 in the section which lists all the 女 characters which have 5-stroke remainders.

This workbook has both a Hanyu Pinyin index and a radical index. Why not get used to how these indexes work by picking a character in the book and seeing if you can find it in both of the indexes?

Many dictionaries also have a pure stroke count index (i.e. ignoring the radical). This is useful if you cannot figure out what the radical of the character is. To use this you must count up all the strokes in the character as a whole and then look the character up under that number (so you would look up 姓 under 8 strokes). As you can imagine, this type of index can leave you with long columns of characters to scan through before you find the one you're looking for, so it's usually a last resort!

All these methods have their pitfalls and complications, so recently a completely new way of looking up characters has been devised. The *Chinese Character Fast Finder* (see the inside back cover) organizes characters purely by their shapes so that you can look up any one of 3,000 characters very quickly without knowing its meaning, radical, pronunciation or stroke count!

How should I use this workbook?
One good way to learn characters is to practice writing them, especially if you think about what each character means as you write it. This will fix the characters in your memory better than if you just look at them without writing them.

If you're working on your own without a teacher, work on a few characters at a time. Go at a pace that suits you; it's much better to do small but regular amounts of writing than to do large chunks at irregular intervals. You might start with just one or two characters each day and increase this as you get better at it. Frequent repetition is the key! Try to get into a daily routine of learning a few new characters and also reviewing the ones you learned on previous days. It's also a good idea to keep a list of which characters you've learned each day, and then to "test yourself" on the characters you learned the previous day, three days ago, a week ago and a month ago. Each time you test yourself they will stay in your memory for a longer period.

But *don't* worry if you can't remember a character you wrote out ten times only yesterday! This is quite normal to begin with. Just keep going—it will all be sinking in without you realizing it.

Once you've learned a few characters you can use flash cards to test yourself on them in a random order. You can make your own set of cards, or use a ready-made set like *Chinese in a Flash* (see the inside back cover).

How do I write the characters?
Finally, let's get down to business and talk about actually writing the characters! Under each character in this book,

the first few boxes show how the character is written, stroke by stroke. There is a correct way to draw each character, and the diagrams in the boxes show you both the order to draw the strokes in, and also the direction for each stroke.

Use the three gray examples to trace over and then carry on by yourself, drawing the characters using the correct stroke order and directions. The varying thicknesses of the lines show you what the characters would look like if they were drawn with a brush, but if you're using a pencil or ball-point pen don't worry about this. Just trace down the middle of the lines and you will produce good hand-written characters.

Pay attention to the length of each of the strokes so that your finished character has the correct proportions. Use the gray dotted lines inside each box as a guide to help you start and end each stroke in the right place.

You may think that it doesn't really matter how the strokes are written as long as the end result looks the same. To some extent this is true, but there are some good reasons for knowing the "proper" way to write the characters. Firstly, it helps you to count strokes, and secondly it will make your finished character "look right", and also help you to read other people's hand-written characters later on. It's better in the long run to learn the correct method of writing the characters from the beginning because, as with so many other things, once you get into "bad" habits it can be very hard to break them!

If you are left-handed, just use your left hand as normal, but still make sure you use the correct stroke order and directions when writing the strokes. For example, draw your horizontal strokes left to right, even if it feels more natural to draw them right to left.

For each Chinese character there is a fixed, correct order in which to write the strokes. But these "stroke orders" do follow some fairly general rules. The main thing to remember is:

- Generally work left to right and top to bottom.

Some other useful guidelines are:

- Horizontal lines are written before vertical ones (see 才, page 52);
- Lines that slope down and to the left are written before those that slope down and to the right (see 分, page 19);
- A central part or vertical line is written before symmetrical or smaller lines at the sides (see 水, page 100);
- The top and sides of an outer box are written first, then whatever is inside the box, then the bottom is written last to "close" it (see 因, page 21).

As you work through the book you'll see these rules in action and get a feel for them, and you'll know how to draw virtually any Chinese character without having to be shown.

Practice, practice, practice!

Your first attempts at writing will be awkward, but as with most things you'll get better with practice. That's why there are lots of squares for you to use. And don't be too hard on yourself (we all draw clumsy-looking characters when we start); just give yourself plenty of time and practice. After a while, you'll be able to look back at your early attempts and compare them with your most recent ones, and see just how much you've improved.

After writing the same character a number of times (a row or two at most), move on to another one. Don't fill up the whole page at one sitting! Then, after writing several other characters, come back later and do a few more of the first one. Can you remember the stroke order without having to look at the diagram?

Finally, try writing out sentences, or lines of different characters, on ordinary paper. To begin with you can mark out squares to write in if you want to, but after that simply imagine the squares and try to keep your characters all equally sized and equally spaced.

Have fun, and remember—the more you practice writing the characters the easier it gets!

歲

suì years old

common words

歲月 **suì yuè** years
歲數 **suì shu** age
幾歲(?) **jǐ suì** how old(?)
同歲 **tóng suì** same age
週歲 **zhōu suì** first birthday; one year old

13 strokes

radical

止

simplified form

岁

怎

zěn how(?); why(?)

common words

怎麼(?) **zěn me** how(?); why(?)

怎麼樣(?) **zěn me yàng** how about it(?)

怎樣(?) **zěn yàng** how about it(?)

怎麼回事(?) **zěn me huí shì** what's going on(?)

怎麼得了 **zěn me dé liǎo** express a serious condition

不怎麼 **bù zěn me** not very

ノ	乍	乍	乍	乍	乍	怎	怎
怎	怎	怎	怎				

樣	common words	15 strokes

様

yàng 1. appearance 2. type

樣子 **yàng zi** look; appearance
樣本 **yàng běn** sample book
一樣/同樣 **yī yàng/tóng yàng** alike
花樣 **huā yàng** 1. variety 2. trick
兩樣/不一樣 **liǎng yàng/bù yī yàng** different
這樣 **zhè yàng** in this way

15 strokes

radical
木

simplified form
样

一	十	才	木	才	术	样	样
样	样	样	样	様	様	様	様
様	様						

12

認

rèn 1. admit
2. recognize; identify

common words

認同/認可 **rèn tóng/rèn kě** approve
認錯 **rèn cuò** admit one's mistake
認為 **rèn wéi** of the opinion
認得 **rèn de** recognize; identify
認輸 **rèn shū** admit defeat
公認 **gōng rèn** acknowledge

14 strokes

radical

言

simplified form

认

丶	二	言	言	言	言	言	訁
訁	訒	認	認	認	認	認	認
認							

識	common words	19 strokes
	識字 **shí zì** literate	
	識別 **shí bié** distinguish; discern	**radical**
	認識 **rèn shi** know each other; recognize	言
	知識 **zhī shi** knowledge	
	常識 **cháng shí** 1. general knowledge 2. common	**simplified form**
shí 1. know; knowledge 2. recognize	sense	识

現

xiàn present; now

common words

現在 **xiàn zài** now; at present
現金 **xiàn jīn** cash
現場 **xiàn chǎng** scene (of happenings)
現成 **xiàn chéng** readymade
表現 **biǎo xiàn** performance
出現 **chū xiàn** appear

11 strokes

radical

玉

simplified form

现

一 1	三 2	王 3	王 4	珏 5	珇 6	珇 7	珇 8
珇 9	珇 10	現 11	現	現	現		

可

kě can; permitted

common words

可以 **kě yǐ** can; permitted
可是 **kě shì** 1. really 2. but
可能 **kě néng** maybe; possible
可口 **kě kǒu** tasty; delicious
可見 **kě jiàn** obviously
可笑 **kě xiào** laughable; funny
還可以 **hái kě yǐ** not bad; all right

一	丆	丁	口	可	可	可	可

點

diǎn 1. o'clock
2. dot; drop 3. point

common words

點頭　**diǎn tóu**　nod
點心　**diǎn xīn**　snack
點菜　**diǎn cài**　order dishes (from a menu)
一點兒/點兒　**yī diǎnr/diǎnr**　a little; a bit
三點/三點鐘　**sān diǎn/sān diǎn zhōng**　three o'clock
雨點　**yǔ diǎn**　raindrops
要點　**yào diǎn**　main point; essential point

17 strokes

radical

黑

simplified form

半

bàn 1. half; mid
2. very little/few

半天 **bàn tiān** 1. half day 2. a long time
半價 **bàn jià** half price
半空 **bàn kōng** in the sky; mid air
九點半 **jiǔ diǎn bàn** half past nine
大半/多半 **dà bàn/dūo bàn** majority
另一半 **lìng yī bàn** other half (of a couple)

5 strokes

radical

十

᠈	᠈᠈	丷	兰	半	半	半	半

分

fēn/fèn 1. minute
2. divide 3. point/mark

common words

分工 **fēn gōng** share work
分别 **fēn bié** 1. split up (work) 2. distinguish
分量 **fèn liàng** amount
分心 **fēn xīn** distract
分手 **fēn shǒu** 1. say goodbye; part 2. break up (a relationship)
五分 **wǔ fēn** five points/marks
五分/五分鐘 **wǔ fēn/wǔ fēn zhōng** five minutes (time)

4 strokes

radical

刀（刂）

ノ	八	分	分	分	分	分	

鐘

zhōng 1. bell 2. clock 3. time (measure)

common words

鐘聲 **zhōng shēng** ringing (of bells)
鐘頭 **zhōng tóu** hour (time)
鐘表 **zhōng biǎo** clocks and watches; timepiece
鐘情 **zhōng qíng** deeply in love
分鐘 **fēn zhōng** minute (time)

20 strokes

radical
金

simplified form
钟

ノ¹	人²	今³	今⁴	午⁵	午⁶	金⁷	金⁸
金⁹	金¹⁰	金¹¹	金¹²	鋅¹³	鋪¹⁴	鎧¹⁵	鎧¹⁶
鎧¹⁷	鐙¹⁸	鐘¹⁹	鐘²⁰	鐘	鐘	鐘	

因

yīn because (of);
cause; reason

common words

因此 **yīn cǐ** so; therefore
因為 **yīn wèi** because (of)
因而 **yīn ér** thus; as a result
原因 **yuán yīn** reason
起因 **qǐ yīn** cause; origin

為

wèi/wéi 1. for; on behalf of 2. do; act as

common words

為了　**wèi le**　in order to; for
為什麼(?)　**wèi shěn me**　why(?); reason
為人　**wéi rén**　a person's conduct/behavior
為生　**wéi shēng**　make a living
為難　**wéi nán**　make things difficult (for somebody)
為期　**wéi qī**　last for a period
為止　**wéi zhǐ**　until ...; up to ...

9 strokes

radical

火（灬）

simplified form

为

很

hěn very

common words

很高	**hěn gāo**	very tall
很矮	**hěn ǎi**	very short (height)
很低	**hěn dī**	very low
很長	**hěn cháng**	very long
很短	**hěn duǎn**	very short (length)
很慢	**hěn màn**	very slow
很快	**hěn kuài**	very fast

9 strokes

radical

彳

忙

máng busy

radical

心（忄）

common words

忙着 **máng zhe** busy with something
忙碌 **máng lù** busy
忙不忙(?) **máng bu máng** busy(?)
太忙了 **tài máng le** too busy
大忙人 **dà máng rén** a very busy person
幫忙 **bāng máng** (to) help; help
急忙 **jí máng** quickly; hastily

忄¹	忄²	忄³	忙⁴	忙⁵	忙⁶	忙	忙
忙							

hái/huán 1. still; yet
2. return; give back

common words	17 strokes
還有 **hái yǒu** furthermore; moreover	**radical**
還是 **hái shi** 1. still 2. had better	辵 (辶)
還好 **hái hǎo** all right; okay	
還要 **hái yào** still want	**simplified form**
還沒 **hái méi** yet to ...	
還書 **huán shū** return book(s)	
還價 **huán jià** counter offer (on pricing)	

喜

xǐ 1. happy 2. fond of 3. pregnancy

common words

喜歡/喜愛 **xǐ huān/xǐ ài** fond of
喜事 **xǐ shì** happy event
喜酒 **xǐ jiǔ** wedding dinner
恭喜 **gōng xǐ** congratulate
有喜 **yóu xǐ** pregnant
可喜 **kě xǐ** heartening

12 strokes

radical

口

一	十	士	古	吉	吉	吉	吉
壹	幸	喜	喜	喜	喜	喜

歡

huān 1. happy
2. vigorous

common words

歡樂/歡喜 **huān lè/huān xǐ** happy; joyful
歡迎 **huān yíng** welcome
歡呼 **huān hū** cheer
歡笑 **huān xiào** laugh heartily
歡送 **huān sòng** see ... off
歡心 **huān xīn** favor; fond feeling

22 strokes

radical

欠

simplified form

欢

等

děng 1. wait 2. type 3. grade; rank

common words

等候/等待　**děng hòu/děng dài**　wait for
等到　**děng dào**　wait until; by the time that ...
等等　**děng děng**　... and so on
等于　**děng yú**　equals to
上等　**shàng děng**　high class
下等　**xià děng**　low grade; inferior
平等　**píng děng**　equal

12 strokes

radical

竹（⺮）

ノ¹	⺅²	⺶³	⺶⁴	竹⁵	竹⁶	竻⁷	笍⁸

笙⁹	笙¹⁰	等¹¹	等¹²	等	等	等

28

太

tài 1. extremely; too
2. senior

common words

太好了　**tài hǎo le** That's great!
太太　**tài tai** 1. wife 2. Mrs
太子　**tài zi** crown prince
太陽　**tài yáng** sun
太空　**tài kōng** space
太平　**tài píng** peaceful
老太太/老太婆　**lǎo tài tai/lǎo tài pó** old woman

4 strokes

radical

大

| 一 | ナ | 大 | 太 | 太 | 太 | 太 | |

久

jiǔ 1. length of time
2. for a long time

common words

久久 **jiǔ jiǔ** for a very long time
久等 **jiǔ děng** wait for a long time
不久 **bù jiǔ** not a very long time; soon
好久 **hǎo jiǔ** a long time
永久 **yǒng jiǔ** forever; permanent
長久 **cháng jiǔ** for a long time

3 strokes

radical

丿

久 久 久 久 久

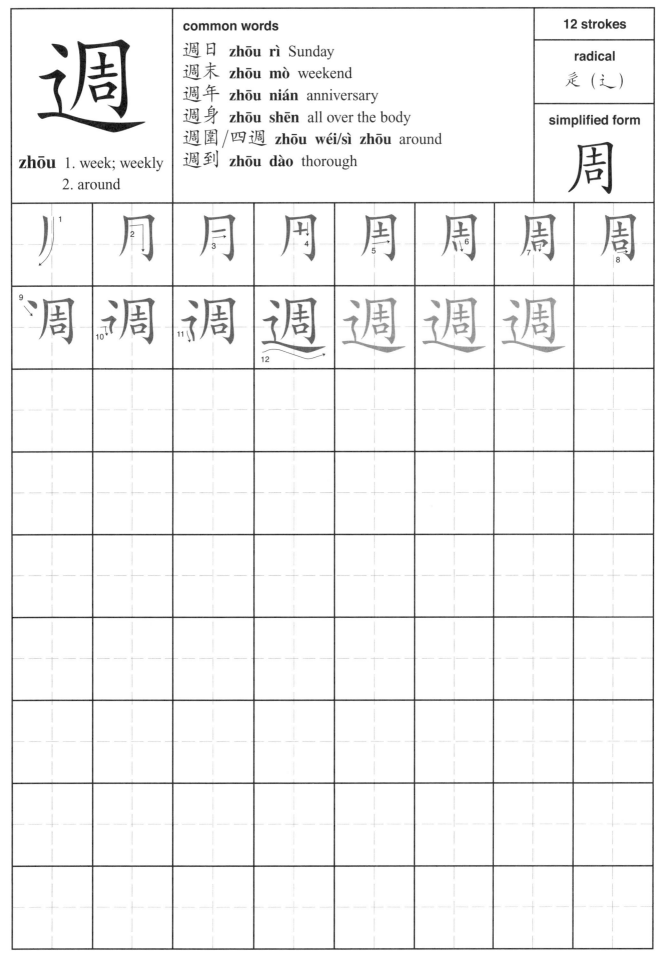

週

zhōu 1. week; weekly
2. around

common words

週日　**zhōu rì** Sunday
週末　**zhōu mò** weekend
週年　**zhōu nián** anniversary
週身　**zhōu shēn** all over the body
週圍/四週　**zhōu wéi/sì zhōu** around
週到　**zhōu dào** thorough

12 strokes

radical

辵（辶）

simplified form

周

末

mò end; last part

common words

末期 **mò qī** last phase
末日 **mò rì** doomsday
末了 **mò liǎo** last; at the end
末尾 **mò wěi** the end
末班車 **mò bān chē** last train; last bus
週末 **zhōu mò** weekend

5 strokes

radical

木

打

dǎ/dá 1. strike 2. send 3. play 4. dozen

common words

打電話 **dǎ diàn huà** make a phone call
打開 **dǎ kāi** open
打架 **dǎ jià** fight
打掃 **dǎ sǎo** clean up
打算 **dǎ suan** intend; plan
打扮 **dǎ bàn** make up; dress up
打油 **dǎ yóu** buy petrol

5 strokes

radical

手（扌）

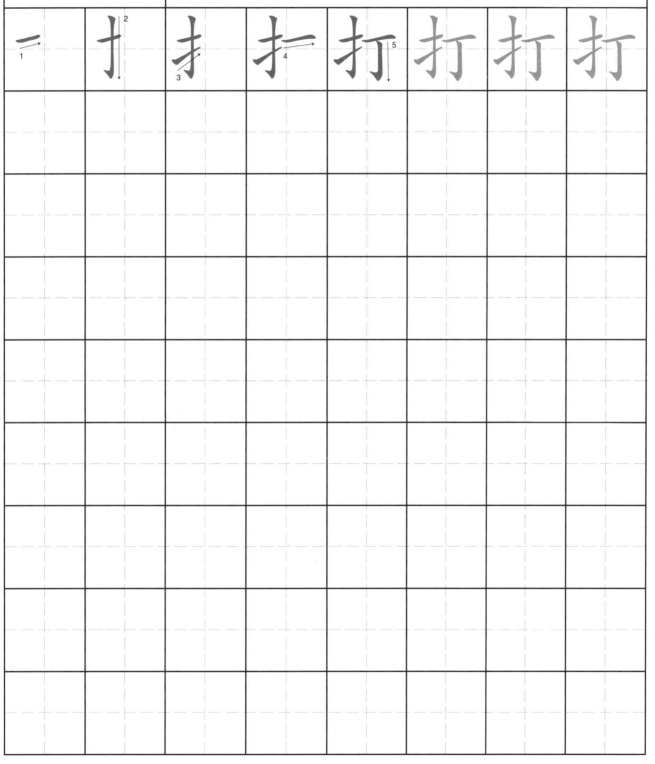

球

qiú 1. ball
2. ball-shaped object

radical

玉

common words

球員 **qiú yuán** player (for a ball game)
球隊 **qiú duì** team (for a ball game)
球場 **qiú chǎng** field; pitch (for a ball game)
球鞋 **qiú xié** sport shoe
打球 **dǎ qiú** play a ball game
藍球 **lán qiú** basketball
足球 **zú qiú** football

一	二	干	王	王	丮	丮	丮
球	球	球	球	球	球		

看

kàn/kān 1. see; watch
2. read 3. look after

common words

看看 **kàn kan** have a look
看見 **kàn jiàn** see
看電影 **kàn diàn yǐng** go for a movie
看不起/小看 **kàn bu qǐ/xiǎo kàn** look down on
看病 **kàn bìng** 1. consult a doctor 2. see a patient
看孩子 **kān hái zi** babysit
難看 **nán kàn** ugly; don't look good

9 strokes

radical

目

書

shū 1. book;
document 2. write

common words

書本 **shū běn** book
書包 **shū bāo** school bag
書店 **shū diàn** bookstore
書房 **shū fáng** study; study room
說明書 **shuō míng shū** instruction manual
圖書館 **tú shū guǎn** library
百科全書 **bǎi kē quán shū** encyclopedia

radical
日

simplified form
书

㇇	三	彐	彐	彐	聿	書	書
書	書	書	書	書			

36

常		common words				11 strokes	

常常/時常 **cháng cháng/shí cháng** frequently
常見 **cháng jiàn** commonplace; ordinary
常年 **cháng nián** all year round
常人 **cháng rén** ordinary person; man in the street
平常 **píng cháng** ordinary; usual
正常 **zhèng cháng** normal; regular
日常 **rì cháng** everyday; daily

cháng 1. often
2. common

radical
巾

丨	丷	业	业	尚	尚	尚	尚
常	常	常	常	常	常		

寫	**common words**				**15 strokes**		
	寫字 **xiě zì** write characters/words				**radical**		
	寫信 **xiě xìn** write a letter				宀		
	寫作 **xiě zuò** writing; composition				**simplified form**		
xiě write; compose	寫生 **xiě shēng** sketch/draw from nature						
	大寫 **dà xiě** upper case; write in capital letters				**写**		
	小寫 **xiǎo xiě** lower case; write in small letters						
	填寫 **tián xiě** fill out (a form)						

電

diàn 1. electricity
2. electric shock

common words

電影　**diàn yǐng** movie; film
電話　**diàn huà** telephone
電冰箱　**diàn bīng xiāng** refrigerator
電燈　**diàn dēng** eletric light
電池　**diàn chí** battery
閃電　**shǎn diàn** lightning
回電　**huí diàn** return a call (reply)

13 strokes

radical

雨

simplified form

視		common words			11 strokes	

視		**common words**			**11 strokes**	
		視力 **shì lì** eyesight; vision			**radical**	
		視為 **shì wéi** see as			示（礻）	
		電視 **diàn shì** 1. television program 2. television set				
		電視機 **diàn shì jī** television set			**simplified form**	
		近視 **jìn shì** myopia; nearsightedness				
shì watch; see		遠視 **yuǎn shì** hyperopia; farsightedness			视	

丶	礻	礻	礻	礻	礻	礻
礻	視	視	視	視	視	

唱

chàng sing

11 strokes

radical

口

common words

唱歌/歌唱　**chàng gē/gē chàng**　sing
唱戲　**chàng xì**　sing an opera
唱片　**chàng piàn**　record; phonograph
合唱　**hé chàng**　sing in chorus
高唱　**gāo chàng**　sing loudly
賣唱　**mài chàng**　sing for a living; busking

歌

gē song

14 strokes

radical

欠

common words

歌星 **gē xīng** star (singer)
歌手 **gē shǒu** singer; vocalist
歌迷 **gē mí** fan of vocalists
國歌 **guó gē** national anthem
兒歌 **ér gē** nursery rhyme
情歌 **qíng gē** love song

一	丂	可	可	可	哥	哥	哥
哥	哥	哥	哥	歌	歌	歌	歌
歌							

吧

ba/bā modal particle

common words

吧臺 **bā tái** bar top
酒吧 **jiǔ bā** pub
好吧 **hǎo ba** Okay!; Fine!
走吧 **zǒu ba** Let's go!
看書吧 **kàn shū ba** Let's read!
再說吧 **zài shuō ba** Let's talk about it later!

7 strokes

radical

口

丨	口	口	叼	吅	叩	吧	吧
吧	吧						

聽

tīng listen; hear

22 strokes

radical
耳

simplified form
听

common words

聽見／聽到 **tīng jiàn/tīng dào** heard
聽話 **tīng huà** obedient
聽寫 **tīng xiě** dictate; dictation
聽説 **tīng shuō** it is said
聽眾 **tīng zhòng** audience; listeners
打聽 **dǎ tīng** ask; inquire

音

yīn sound; tone

common words

音樂 **yīn yuè** music
音樂會 **yīn yuè huì** concert
音樂家 **yīn yuè jiā** musician
聲音 **shēng yīn** sound; voice
發音／讀音 **fā yīn/dú yīn** pronunciation
口音 **kǒu yīn** accent

9 strokes

radical

音

丶	二	六	立	立	产	音	音
音	音	音	音				

樂

yuè/lè 1. music
2. happy

common words

樂隊 **yuè duì** band; orchestra
樂器 **yuè qì** musical instrument
樂意 **lè yì** wiling to; ready to
樂園 **lè yuán** paradise
快樂 **kuài lè** happy
歡樂 **huān lè** happy; joyful

15 strokes

radical

木

simplified form

乐

會

huì 1. can; able to
2. meet; meeting

common words

會不會(?) **huì bu huì** know how to(?); able to(?)
會話 **huì huà** conversation; dialog
會合 **huì hé** assemble; meet
開會 **kāi huì** hold a meeting
約會 **yuē huì** date; appointment
機會 **jī huì** opportunity

13 strokes

radical

日

simplified form

会

跳

tiào 1. jump; bounce
2. beat

common words

跳高 **tiào gāo** high jump
跳遠 **tiào yuǎn** broad jump
跳水 **tiào shuǐ** dive
跳傘 **tiào sǎn** 1. skydive 2. parachute
跳班 **tiào bān** skip a grade/level
心跳 **xīn tiào** heart palpitation; heartbeat

13 strokes

radical

足（⻊）

舞

wǔ dance

common words

舞伴　**wǔ bàn**　dancing partner
舞會　**wǔ huì**　ball (dance)
舞臺　**wǔ tái**　stage
跳舞　**tiào wǔ**　(to) dance
歌舞　**gē wǔ**　song and dance
芭蕾舞　**bā lěi wǔ**　ballet

⺊¹	⺁²	⺁³	午⁴	缶⁵	缶⁶	無⁷
無⁸	舞⁹	舞¹⁰	舞¹¹	舞¹²	舞¹³	舞¹⁴	舞	舞
舞						

對

duì 1. correct 2. treat 3. compare; check

common words

對不起 **duì bu qǐ** 1. sorry 2. excuse me
對手 **duì shǒu** opponent
對方 **duì fāng** other side; other party
對白 **duì bái** dialog (in a play/film)
不對 **bù duì** 1. wrong 2. odd
反對 **fǎn duì** diagree; against
作對 **zuò duì** oppose

14 strokes

radical
寸

simplified form
对

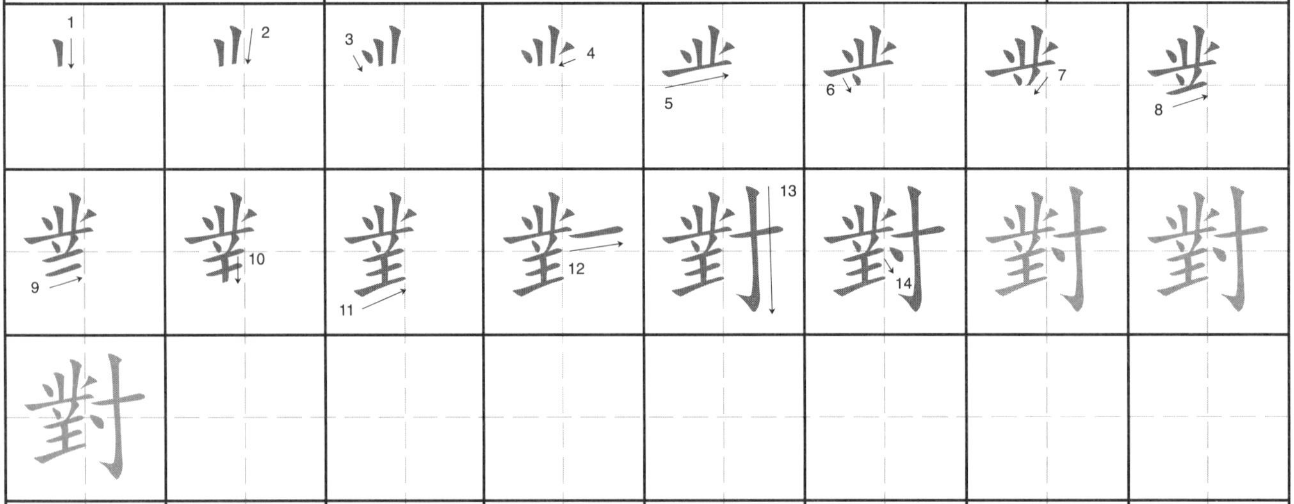

錯

cuò mistaken; wrong

common words

錯字 **cuò zì** incorrectly written characters/words
錯過 **cuò guò** miss (a chance)
不錯 **bù cuò** not bad; pretty good
沒錯 **méi cuò** not wrong; correct
做錯 **zuò cuò** do wrongly
寫錯 **xiě cuò** write wrongly
弄錯/搞錯 **nòng cuò/gǎo cuò** misunderstand

16 strokes

radical

金

simplified form

错

ノ¹	𠆢²	今³	今⁴	全⁵	全⁶	金⁷	金⁸
金⁹	針¹⁰	釧¹¹	錯¹²	錯¹³	錯¹⁴	錯¹⁵	錯¹⁶
錯	錯	錯					

才

cái 1. only 2. talented
3. substance

common words

才四歲 **cái sì suì** only four years old
才能 **cái néng** talent; ability
剛才/方才 **gāng cái/fāng cái** just now
口才 **kǒu cái** eloquence
人才 **rén cái** talented person
天才 **tiān cái** genius

3 strokes

radical

手（扌）

一 才 才 才 才 才

	common words	**6 strokes**
回	回家 **huí jiā** return home 回來 **huí lái** come back 回答 **huí dá** answer 回想 **huí xiǎng** recollect 下回 **xià huí** next time 拿回 **ná huí** take back; recover	**radical** 口

huí 1. return 2. turn around

去

qù 1. go to 2. remove; get rid of

common words

去年 **qù nián** last year
去世 **qù shì** pass away; dead
去過 **qù guò** been to (a place)
回去 **huí qù** return; go back
出去 **chū qù** go out
過去 **guò qù** in the past
失去 **shī qù** lose

一 十 土 去 去 去 去 去

所

suǒ 1. place (location)
2. measure word

common words

所有 **suǒ yǒu** 1. all 2. (one) owns/possesses
所在 **suǒ zài** located; location
廁所 **cè suǒ** toilet; bathroom
住所 **zhù suǒ** residence
診所 **zhěn suǒ** clinic
兩所醫院 **liǎng suǒ yī yuàn** two hospitals

8 strokes

radical

户

ⸯ	厂	戶	戶	戶	所	所	所
所	所	所					

以

yǐ 1. use; by means of
2. according to; because

radical

人

common words

以為 **yǐ wéi** think; believe
以後 **yǐ hòu** afterward; after
以前 **yǐ qián** before; previously
以及 **yǐ jí** and; as well as
以上 **yǐ shàng** above; onward
以外 **yǐ wài** excluding; beyond
所以 **suǒ yǐ** therefore

丨	レ	レ゙	以	以	以	以	以

裡	**common words**	**12 strokes**

裡面/裡邊/裡頭 **lǐ miàn/lǐ bian/lǐ tou** in; inside
家裡 **jiā lǐ** in (one's) home/family
房裡 **fáng lǐ** in the room
屋裡 **wū lǐ** in the house
心裡 **xīn lǐ** in the heart; mental state
鄰裡 **lín lǐ** neighborhood

lǐ in; inside; within

radical
衣（衤）

simplified form
里

外

wài 1. relatives of one's mother 2. outside

common words

外孫 **wài sūn** daughter's son
外婆 **wài pó** grandmother (maternal)
外人 **wài rén** outsider
外賣 **wài mài** take away (service)
門外 **mén wài** outside the gate/door
課外 **kè wài** extracurricular

5 strokes

radical

夕

ノ	夕	夕	夘	外	外	外	外

祇

zhǐ only

common words

祇好/祇得 **zhǐ hǒu/zhǐ dé** have to; must
祇是 **zhǐ shì** only
祇不過 **zhǐ bu guò** 1. only 2. but
祇要 **zhǐ yào** so long as; provided that
祇有 **zhǐ yǒu** only
不祇 **bù zhǐ** not only; not just

9 strokes

radical

衣（衤）

simplified form

只

`	`	衤	衤	衤	衤	祇	祇
祇	祇	祇	祇				

想

xiǎng 1. think
2. reckon 3. want to

common words

想想看 **xiǎng xiǎng kàn** think about it
想起 **xiǎng qǐ** remember; recall
想要 **xiǎng yào** want to; wish for; feel like
想出/想到 **xiǎng chū/xiǎng dào** figure out; think of
想不到 **xiǎng bu dào** unexpected
猜想 **cāi xiǎng** guess; suppose

13 strokes

radical

心

一	十	才	木	机	相	相	相

相	相	想	想	想	想	想	想

玩

wán play

common words

玩耍/遊玩 **wán shuǎ/yóu wán** play
玩具 **wán jù** toy
玩弄 **wán nòng** 1. toy with 2. trick; flirt
開玩笑 **kāi wán xiào** (to) joke
好玩 **hào wán** love to play
好玩 **hǎo wán** fun; entertaining

8 strokes

radical

玉

一	三	王	王	王	王	玡	玩
玩	玩	玩					

愛

ài 1. love 2. enjoy

common words

愛好　**ài hào**　hobby
愛心　**ài xīn**　affection
愛上　**ài shàng**　fall in love with
愛上網　**ài shàng wǎng**　enjoy surfing (internet)
愛人　**ài ren**　1. spouse 2. lover
可愛　**kě ài**　cute; adorable

13 strokes

radical

心

simplified form

爱

睡

shuì sleep

common words

睡醒 **shuì xǐng** wake up
睡衣 **shuì yī** pajamas
睡着 **shuì zháo** fall asleep
睡飽 **shuì bǎo** had a good sleep
想睡 **xiǎng shuì** feel like sleeping
打瞌睡 **dǎ kē shuì** dozing off

覺

jiào/jué 1. sleep
2. feel

common words

睡覺　**shuì jiào**　sleep; go to bed
午覺　**wǔ jiào**　afternoon nap
覺得　**jué de**　feel
發覺　**fā jué**　discover; realize
錯覺　**cuò jué**　illusion; misconception
不知不覺　**bù zhī bù jué**　unconciously

20 strokes

radical
見

simplified form

觉

找

zhǎo 1. look for
2. return change (money)

common words

找到 **zhǎo dào** find; found
找人 **zhǎo rén** look for someone
找出 **zhǎo chū** found out
找尋 **zhǎo xún** search
找錢 **zhǎo qián** return change
找工作/找事作 **zhǎo gōng zuò/zhǎo shì zuò** look for a job

7 strokes

radical

手（扌）

一	扌	扌	扩	扎	找	找
找	找					

到

dào 1. arrive 2. go
3. until

common words

到了　**dào le**　arrived
到處　**dào chù**　everywhere
得到　**dé dào**　get; achieve
拿到　**ná dào**　get hold of
說到　**shuō dào**　touch on; refer to
遲到　**chí dào**　(arrive) late
回到　**huí dào**　return to

8 strokes

radical

刀（刂）

一	工	云	云	至	至	到	到
到	到	到					

		common words				**3 strokes**	

工

gōng 1. work
2. worker (in short)

common words

工人/員工 **gōng rén/yuán gōng** worker
工作 **gōng zuò** 1. (to) work 2. job; work
工具 **gōng jù** tool
工廠 **gōng chǎng** factory
工錢/工資 **gōng qian/gōng zī** pay; wage
停工 **tíng gōng** stop work
做工/打工 **zuò gōng/dǎ gōng** (to) work

3 strokes

radical

工

作

zuò/zuō 1. do
2. write 3. feel

radical

人（亻）

common words

作樂 **zuò lè** enjoy oneself
作弄 **zuō nòng** tease; make fun
作業 **zuò yè** homework; task
作家/作者 **zuò jiā/zuò zhě** composer; author
作客 **zuò kè** be a guest
合作 **hé zuò** cooperate
當作 **dāng zuò** regard as; consider to be

亻 亻 亻 作 作 作 作 作

作 作

後

hòu 1. back; behind
2. after; later

common words

後來/然後 **hòu lái/rán hòu** afterward; and then
後面/後邊 **hòu miàn/hòu bian** back; behind
後門 **hòu mén** back door
後天 **hòu tiān** day after tomorrow
後父 **hòu fù** stepfather
今後 **jīn hòu** from now on
最後 **zuì hòu** 1. (the) last 2. finally; at last

9 strokes

radical

彳

simplified form

后

快

kuài fast; quickly; hurry up

common words

快樂/愉快 **kuài lè/yú kuài** happy; joyful
快餐 **kuài cān** fast food
快要/快了 **kuài yào/kuài le** soon
快點兒/趕快 **kuài diǎnr/gǎn kuài** hurry up; quickly
快車 **kuài chē** express bus/train
加快 **jiā kuài** accelerate
外快 **wài kuài** supplementary income

7 strokes

radical

心（忄）

丿¹	忄²	忄³	忄⁴	忄⁵	快⁶	快⁷

快	快					

放

fàng 1. release
2. place; lay

放心 **fàng xīn** at ease
放手 **fàng shǒu** let go
放下 **fàng xià** lay down; let go
放假 **fàng jià** (take) vacation
放屁 **fàng pì** 1. break wind 2. talk nonsense
放開 **fàng kāi** release; set free
放火 **fàng huǒ** 1. set fire 2. commit arson

8 strokes

radical

攵

丶	二	亠	方	方	方	放	放
放	放	放					

71

開

kāi 1. open 2. bloom
3. operate; turn on

common words

開心 **kāi xīn** happy
開花／開放 **kāi huā/kāi fàng** (to) flower
開車 **kāi chē** drive a car
走開 **zǒu kāi** leave; get lost
分開 **fēn kāi** separate
打開 **dǎ kāi** open
白開水 **bái kāi shuǐ** boiled water

12 strokes

radical

門

simplified form

开

丨	冂	冃	冃	門	門	門	門
門	門	開	開	開	開	開	

意

yì 1. meaning 2. idea

common words

意見 **yì jiàn** opinion; view
意外 **yì wài** 1. accident 2. unexpected
注意 **zhù yì** pay attention; note
同意 **tóng yì** agree; accept
有意/故意 **yǒu yì/gù yì** purposely
大意 **dà yì** 1. careless 2. main meaning/idea
得意 **dé yì** complacent

13 strokes

radical

心

亠	二	六	立	立	产	音	音
音	音	意	意	意	意	意	意

思

sī think of; consider; ponder

common words

思想 **sī xiǎng** thinking; ideology
思考 **sī kǎo** think over; ponder
意思 **yì si** meaning
有意思 **yǒu yì si** interesting
沒意思 **méi yì si** not interesting; meaningless
小意思 **xiǎo yì si** 1. That's easy! 2. small token
心思 **xīn si** 1. thinking 2. mood

9 strokes

radical

心

說		**common words**				14 strokes	
		説明 **shuō míng** explain				radical	
		説話 **shuō huà** speak				言	
		説不定 **shuō bu dìng** perhaps; may be					
		説大話 **shuō dà huà** (to) boast				**simplified form**	
		説謊 **shuō huǎng** (to) lie					
shuō speak		愛説笑 **ài shuō xiào** love to joke				说	
		小説 **xiǎo shuō** novel					

丶	二	三	言	言	言	言	言
訁	訁	詒	詒	詍	説	説	説
説							

空

kòng/kōng 1. sky
2. empty 3. free

common words

空白 **kòng bái** blank
空位 **kòng wèi** empty seat
空氣 **kōng qì** air
空中 **kōng zhōng** mid-air
天空 **tiān kōng** sky
有空 **yǒu kòng** free

8 strokes

radical

穴

話

huà (one's) words

common words

話題　**huà tí**　subject (of a conversation)
話劇　**huà jù**　stage play
笑話　**xiào huà**　joke
壞話　**huài huà**　malicious talk
電話　**diàn huà**　telephone
空話　**kōng huà**　empty talk; idle talk

13 strokes

radical
言

simplified form
话

要

yào/yāo 1. need
2. want 3. ask for

common words

要是 **yào shì** if
要好 **yào hǎo** on good terms, befriend
要求 **yāo qiú** request
要不/要不然 **yào bù/yào bu rán** otherwise; or else
要緊/重要 **yào jǐn/zhòng yào** important
就要 **jiù yào** about to
須要 **xū yào** need to

9 strokes

radical

西 （西）

知

zhī know; knowledge

common words

知道 **zhī dào** know
知己 **zhī jǐ** bosom friend
明知 **míng zhī** know fully well
得知 **dé zhī** know/learn about
已知 **yǐ zhī** already known
通知／告知 **tōng zhī/gào zhī** notify; inform

8 strokes

radical

矢

ノ¹	㇍²	㇍³	𠂉⁴	矢⁵	知⁶	知⁷	知⁸
知	知	知					

道

dào 1. road; way
2. moral

common words

道歉 **dào qiàn** apologize
道謝 **dào xiè** (to) thank
道別 **dào bié** bid farewell; part
道理 **dào li** reasoning; doctrine
道路 **dào lù** road
味道 **wèi dào** taste; flavor
街道 **jiē dào** street

13 strokes

radical

辵 (辶)

丷	丷	兰	兰	芹	首	首	首
首	首	首	道	道	道	道	道

別

bié/biè 1. part
2. tuck 3. don't

common words

別的 **bié de** other
別人 **bié rén** other people
別處 **bié chù** elsewhere
別忘了 **bié wàng le** don't forget
別客氣 **bié kè qi** you're welcome; not at all
特別 **tè bié** special

7 strokes

radical

刀（刂）

simplified form

別

丿	口	口	另	吊	別	別	別
別	別					

客

kè guest

common words

客人　**kè rén**　guest
客户　**kè hù**　customer
客廳　**kè tīng**　living room
客房　**kè fáng**　guest room
客氣　**kè qi**　courteous; polite
常客　**cháng kè**　regular customer
乘客　**chéng kè**　passenger

丶	宀	宀	宀	宀	宀	客
客	客	客	客			

氣

qì 1. gas 2. angry

common words

氣死/氣死人　**qì sǐ/qì sǐ rén**　enraged
氣味　**qì wèi**　smell
氣球　**qì qiú**　balloon
氣候　**qì hòu**　weather
氣力　**qì lì**　strength
生氣　**shēng qì**　angry
小氣　**xiǎo qì**　1. stingy; mean 2. in poor taste

10 strokes

radical

气

simplified form

气

進

jìn 1. enter
2. progress

common words

進去/進入 **jìn qù/jìn rù** go in; enter; get inside
進來 **jìn lái** come in
進步 **jìn bù** show improvement
進行 **jìn xíng** carry out (an event)
上進 **shàng jìn** make progress
改進 **gǎi jìn** improve
先進 **xiān jìn** advanced

12 strokes

radical

辵 (辶)

simplified form

进

ノ¹	イ²	イ³	イ⁴	イ⁵	イ⁶	イ⁷	隹⁸
隹⁹	谁¹⁰	谁¹¹	進¹²	進	進	進	

來

lái 1. come 2. appear

radical

人

simplified form

来

common words

來到 **lái dào** arrive
來不及 **lái bu jí** too late; cannot make it
起來 **qǐ lái** get up; rise
看來 **kàn lái** look like; appear to be
本來 **běn lái** at first; originally
從來 **cóng lái** all along; never
原來如此 **yuán lái rú cǐ** I see, that's way

一	厂	丞	巫	巫	來	來	來
來	來	來					

坐

zuò 1. sit 2. ride; travel by

common words

坐下 **zuò xià** sit down
坐位 **zuò wèi** seat
坐牢 **zuò láo** imprison
坐飛機 **zuò fēi jī** travel by air/plane
坐船 **zuò chuán** travel by sea/boat
乘坐 **chéng zuò** travel by
靜坐 **jìng zuò** sit in silence

呀

yā/ya 1. creeking
2. sentence-ending particle

common word

哎呀！/呀！ **aī yā/yā** Oh!; Ah! (expresses surprise, annoyance, reluctance, etc)

來呀！ **lái ya** Please come!

丨	口	口	叮	叮	呀	呀	呀
呀	呀						

介

jiè between

common words

介紹 **jiè shào** (to) introduce

介意 **jiè yì** mind

介詞 **jiè cí** preposition (grammar)

介入 **jiè rù** get involved; interfere

不介意 **bù jiè yì** don't mind

4 strokes

radical

人

紹

shào join together; connect

common words

介紹／紹介 **jiè shào／shào jiè** (to) introduce
介紹信 **jiè shào xìn** letter of introduction

高

gāo 1. tall; high
2. senior

common words

高等 **gāo děng** high level
高大 **gāo dà** 1. huge 2. glorious
高矮 **gāo ǎi** height
高低 **gāo dī** 1. height 2. difference (in height/degree)
高地 **gāo dì** highland
高見 **gāo jiàn** opinion
高手 **gāo shǒu** expert

亠 亠 亠 亠 亠 亠 高 高

高 高 高 高 高

興

xìng/xīng 1. prosper
2. excitement; happy

common words

興趣 **xìng qù** interest
興奮 **xīng fèn** excited
興奮劑 **xīng fèn jì** stimulant
興衝衝 **xīng chōng chōng** happily
高興 **gāo xìng** happy
掃興 **sǎo xīng** disappointed

15 strokes

radical

臼

simplified form

兴

漂

piāo/piǎo/piào

1. float; drift 2. rinse

14 strokes

radical

水 (氵)

common words

漂亮 **piào liang** beautiful; wonderful; outstanding
漂白 **piǎo bái** bleach
漂流 **piāo liú** drift
漂浮 **piāo fú** float

亮

liàng 1. bright
2. show

common words

亮光 **liàng guāng** light
亮晶晶 **liàng jīng jīng** sparkle
明亮 **míng liàng** bright; shiny
月亮 **yuè liàng** moon
發亮 **fā liàng** glow
照亮 **zhào liàng** illuminate

9 strokes

radical

亠

simplified form

亮

丶	二	亠	市	古	亩	高	亮

亮	亮	亮	亮			

口		**common words**			3 strokes	
		口紅 **kǒu hóng** lipstick			**radical**	
		口袋 **kǒu dai** pocket			口	
		口氣 **kǒu qì** tone (when saying something)				
		胃口 **wèi kǒu** 1. appetite 2. liking (in food)				
		門口 **mén kǒu** doorway				
kǒu 1. mouth		入口 **rù kǒu** entrance				
2. entrance; opening		窗口 **chuāng kǒu** window				

渴

kě 1. thirsty 2. eagerly

common words

渴求 **kě qiú** hunger for
渴望 **kě wàng** long for
口渴 **kǒu kě** thirsty
又渴又饿 **yòu kě yòu è** hungry and thirsty

12 strokes

radical

水（氵）

丶	氵	氵	氵	氵	氵	渇	渇
渴	渴	渴	渴	渴	渴	渴	

喝

hē/hè 1. drink
2. shout

common words

喝水　**hē shuǐ**　drink water
喝茶　**hē chá**　drink tea
喝酒　**hē jiǔ**　drink alcohol
喝醉　**hē zuì**　drunk
喝彩　**hè cǎi**　applaud; cheer
請喝　**qǐng hē**　please drink
好喝　**hǎo hē**　taste good (drinks)

12 strokes

radical

口

茶

chá tea

radical

艸 (艹)

simplified form

茶

common words

茶點　**chá diǎn**　refreshments
茶葉　**chá yè**　tea leaves
茶具　**chá jù**　tea set
茶壺　**chá hú**　teapot
泡茶　**pào chá**　make tea
倒茶　**dào chá**　pour tea
奶茶　**nǎi chá**　milk tea

給

gěi 1. give 2. allow 3. for 4. ...to

common words

給以 **gěi yǐ** give
給忘了 **gěi wàng le** forgotten
送給 **sòng gěi** give as a present
賣給 **mài gěi** sell to
借給 **jiè gěi** lend to
嫁給 **jià gěi** marry to (a man)

12 strokes

radical
糸

simplified form

给

杯

bēi 1. cup
2. measure word

radical

木

common words

杯子 **bēi zi** cup
茶杯 **chá bēi** teacup
世界杯 **shì jiè bēi** World Cup
一杯冷水 **yī bēi lěng shuǐ** a glass of cold water
两杯咖啡 **liǎng bēi kā fēi** two cups of coffee
三杯熱茶 **sān bēi rè chá** three cups of hot tea

水

shuǐ 1. water 2. liquid

common words

水果 **shuǐ guǒ** fruit
水牛 **shuǐ niú** water buffalo
水池 **shuǐ chí** pond
汗水 **hàn shuǐ** sweat
汽水 **qì shuǐ** fizzy drink
薪水 **xīn shuǐ** salary
香水 **xiāng shuǐ** perfume

亅 刁 水 水 水 水 水

就

jiù 1. and then; then
2. only

common words

就是 **jiù shì** 1. exactly 2. even (though) 3. only
就要 **jiù yào** about to
就算 **jiù suàn** even if
就讀 **jiù dú** study
就任 **jiù rèn** take office
成就 **chéng jiù** achievement

起

qǐ 1. rise
2. happen 3. begin

common words

起來／起身 **qǐ lái/qǐ shēn** get up; rise
起飛 **qǐ fēi** take off
起火 **qǐ huǒ** catch fire
拿起 **ná qǐ** pick up
看不起 **kàn bu qǐ** despise; look down on
對不起 **duì bu qǐ** 1. sorry 2. excuse me
了不起 **liǎo bu qǐ** terrific; incredible

10 strokes

radical

走

simplified form

起

牀			common words				8 strokes

common words

牀單 **chuáng dān** bedsheet
牀上 **chuáng shàng** on the bed
上牀 **shàng chuáng** go to bed
起牀 **qǐ chuáng** get out (of bed)
雙人牀 **shuāng rén chuáng** double bed
單人牀 **dān rén chuáng** single bed
一牀棉被 **yī chuáng mián bèi** a quilt

chuáng 1. bed
2. measure word

radical
爿

simplified form
床

103

考		common words			6 strokes
		考題 **kǎo tí** test/exam question			**radical**
		考生 **kǎo shēng** examinee			老
kǎo 1. test/exam		考上 **kǎo shàng** pass a test/exam			
2. study; investigate		考慮 **kǎo lǜ** consider			
		考古學 **kǎo gǔ xué** archeology			
		補考 **bǔ kǎo** resit a test/exam			

二	𠂤	土	耂	考	考	考	考
考							

試	**common words**
shì 1. try; test 2. trial; experiment	試試/試試看 **shì shì/shì shì kàn** try and see 試用 **shì yòng** try out 試驗 **shì yàn** experiment 考試 **kǎo shì** test/exam 口試 **kǒu shì** oral exam 嘗試 **cháng shì** try

13 strokes

radical

言

simplified form

试

方

fāng 1. square (shape)
2. prescription

common words

方法 **fāng fǎ** method
方向 **fāng xiàng** direction
四方 **sì fāng** 1. square 2. all directions
西方 **xī fāng** west; western
大方 **dà fang** 1. generous 2. elegant
地方 **dì fāng** 1. place 2. part

4 strokes

radical

方

便

biàn/pián 1. casual 2. then 3. excretion

common words

便飯　**biàn fàn**　quick meal
便當　**biàn dāng**　lunch box
便宜　**pián yi**　cheap
方便　**fāng biàn**　1. convenient 2. appropriate 3. relieve oneself
以便　**yǐ biàn**　in order to; so that
隨便　**suí biàn**　do as one likes; casual

9 strokes

radical

人（亻）

幫

bāng 1. (to) help
2. measure word

common words

幫忙/幫助 **bāng máng/bāng zhù** (to) help; help
幫不上忙 **bāng bù shàng máng** unable to help
幫手 **bāng shǒu** assistant
幫兇 **bāng xiōng** accomplice
四幫人 **sì bāng rén** four gang of people

17 strokes

radical
巾

simplified form
帮

助

zhù (to) help; help

radical

力

common words

助手/助理 **zhù shǒu/zhù lǐ** assistant

助詞 **zhù cí** auxiliary word

幫助 **bāng zhù** (to) help; help

救助 **jiù zhù** relieve; help

贊助 **zàn zhù** sponsor

助人為樂 **zhù rén wéi lè** take pleasure in helping others

丨	冂	目	目	且	耵	助	助
助	助						

Hanyu Pinyin Index

huán shū	還書	25
huān sòng	歡送	27
huān xǐ	歡喜	26
huān xiào	歡笑	27
huān xīn	歡心	27
huān yíng	歡迎	27
huí	回	53
huì	會	47
huì bu huì	會不會(?)	47
huí dá	回答	53
huí dào	回到	66
huí diàn	回電	39
huì hé	會合	47
huì huà	會話	47
huí jiā	回家	53
huí lái	回來	53
huí qù	回去	54
huí xiǎng	回想	53

J

jī huì	機會	47
jí máng	急忙	24
jǐ suì	幾歲(?)	10
jià gěi	嫁給	98
jiā kuài	加快	70
jiā lǐ	家裡	57
jiào/jué	覺	64
jiè	介	88
jiè cí	介詞	88
jiē dào	街道	80
jiè gěi	借給	98
jiè rù	介入	88
jiè shào	介紹	88/89
jiè shào xìn	介紹信	89
jiè yì	介意	88
jìn	進	84
jìn bù	進步	84
jīn hòu	今後	69
jìn lái	進來	84
jìn qù	進去	84
jìn rù	進入	84
jìn shì	近視	40
jìn xíng	進行	84
jìng zuò	靜坐	86
jué/jiào	覺	64
jiǔ	久	30

jiù	就	101
jiǔ bā	酒吧	43
jiǔ děng	久等	30
jiù diǎn bàn	九點半	18
jiù dú	就讀	101
jiǔ jiǔ	久久	30
jiù rèn	就任	101
jiù shì	就是	101
jiù suàn	就算	101
jiù yào	就要	78/101
jiù zhù	救助	109
jué de	覺得	64

K

kāi	開	72
kāi chē	開車	72
kāi fàng	開放	72
kāi huā	開花	72
kāi huì	開會	47
kāi wán xiào	開玩笑	61
kāi xīn	開心	72
kàn/kān	看	35
kàn bìng	看病	35
kàn bu qǐ	看不起	35/102
kàn diàn yǐng	看電影	35
kān hái zi	看孩子	35
kàn jiàn	看見	35
kàn kan	看看	35
kàn lái	看來	85
kàn shū ba	看書吧	43
kǎo	考	104
kǎo gǔ xué	考古學	104
kǎo lù	考慮	104
kǎo shàng	考上	104
kǎo shēng	考生	104
kǎo shì	考試	105
kǎo tí	考題	104
kě	可	16
kě	渴	95
kè	客	82
kě ài	可愛	62
kè fáng	客房	82
kè hù	客戶	82
kě jiàn	可見	16
kě kǒu	可口	16
kě néng	可能	16

kè qi	客氣	82
kě qiú	渴求	95
kè rén	客人	82
kě shì	可是	16
kè tīng	客廳	82
kè wài	課外	58
kě wàng	渴望	95
kě xǐ	可喜	26
kě xiào	可笑	16
kě yǐ	可以	16
kòng/kōng	空	76
kòng bái	空白	76
kōng huà	空話	77
kōng qì	空氣	76
kòng wèi	空位	76
kōng zhōng	空中	76
kǒu	口	94
kǒu cái	口才	52
kǒu dai	口袋	94
kǒu hóng	口紅	94
kǒu kě	口渴	95
kǒu qì	口氣	94
kǒu shì	口試	105
kǒu yīn	口音	45
kuài	快	70
kuài cān	快餐	70
kuài chē	快車	70
kuài diǎnr	快點兒	70
kuài le	快了	70
kuài lè	快樂	46/70
kuài yào	快要	70

L

lái	來	85
lái bu jí	來不及	85
lái dào	來到	85
lái ya	來呀	87
lán qiú	藍球	34
lǎo tài pó	老太婆	29
lǎo tài tai	老太太	29
lè/yuè	樂	46
lè yì	樂意	46
lè yuán	樂園	46
lǐ	裡	57
lǐ bian	裡邊	57
lǐ miàn	裡面	57

Radical Index

1 stroke

[丿]

久   jiǔ   30

2 strokes

[亠]

亮   liàng   93

人 [亻]

以   yǐ   56
作   zuò/zuō   68
來   lái   85
介   jiè   88
便   biàn/pián   107

[十]

半   bàn   18

[厶]

去   qù   54

刀 [刂]

分   fēn/fèn   19
到   dào   66
別   bié/biè   81

[力]

助   zhù   109

3 strokes

[口]

可   kě   16
喜   xǐ   26
唱   chàng   41
吧   ba/bā   43
呀   yā/ya   87
口   kǒu   94
喝   hē/hè   96

[土]

坐   zuò   86

[夕]

外   wài   58

[囗]

因   yīn   21
回   huí   53

[大]

太   tài   29

[宀]

寫   xiě   38
客   kè   82

[寸]

對   duì   50

[工]

工   gōng   67

[巾]

常   cháng   37
幫   bāng   108

[彳]

很   hěn   23
後   hòu   69

[尤]

就   jiù   101

4 strokes

心 [忄]

怎   zěn   11
忙   máng   24
想   xiǎng   60

愛   ài   62
快   kuài   70
意   yì   73
思   sī   74

[戶]

所   suǒ   55

[日]

書   shū   36
會   huì   47

手 [扌]

打   dǎ/dá   33
才   cái   52
找   zhǎo   65

[攴]

放   fàng   71

[方]

方   fāng   106

[木]

樣   yàng   12
末   mò   32
樂   yuè/lè   46
杯   bēi   99

[止]

歲   suì   10

[气]

氣   qì   83

水 [氵]

漂   piāo/piǎo/piào   92
渴   kě   95
水   shuǐ   100

火 [灬]
為   wèi/wéi   22

[欠]
歡   huān   27
歌   gē   42

[爿]
牀   chuáng   103

5 strokes

[玉]
現   xiàn   15
球   qiú   34
玩   wán   61

[目]
看   kàn/kān   35
睡   shuì   63

示 [礻]
視   shì   40

[矢]
知   zhī   79

[穴]
空   kòng/kōng   76

6 strokes

竹 [⺮]
等   děng   28

[糸]
紹   shào   89
給   gěi   98

[老]
考   kǎo   104

[耳]
聽   tīng   44

[臼]
興   xìng/xīng   91

[舛]
舞   wǔ   49

艸 [艹]
茶   chá   97

衣 [衤]
裡   lǐ   57
祇   zhǐ   59

西 [覀]
要   yào/yāo   78

7 strokes

[見]
覺   jiào/jué   64

[言]
認   rèn   13
識   shí   14
說   shuō   75
話   huà   77
試   shì   105

[走]
起   qǐ   102

足 [⻊]
跳   tiào   48

辵 [辶]
還   hái/huán   25
週   zhōu   31
道   dào   80
進   jìn   84

8 strokes

[金]
鐘   zhōng   20
錯   cuò   51

[門]
開   kāi   72

[雨]
電   diàn   39

9 strokes

[音]
音   yīn   45

10 strokes

[高]
高   gāo   90

12 strokes

[黑]
點   diǎn   17

English–Chinese Index

A

a quilt 一牀棉被 yī chuáng mián bèi *103*
a glass of cold water 一杯冷水 yī bēi lěng shuǐ *99*
a little/a bit 一點兒/點兒 yī diǎnr/diǎnr *17*
a long time 半天 bàn tiān *18*; 好久 hǎo jiǔ *30*
ability 才能 cái néng *52*
able to 會 huì *47*
able to(?) 會不會(?) huì bu huì *47*
about to 就要 jiù yào *78, 101*
above 以上 yǐ shàng *56*
accelerate 加快 jiā kuài *70*
accent 口音 kǒu yīn *45*
accident 意外 yì wài *73*
accomplice 幫兇 bāng xiōng *108*
according to 以 yǐ *56*
achieve 得到 dé dào *66*
achievement 成就 chéng jiù *101*
acknowledge 公認 gōng rèn *13*
act as 為 wéi *22*
admit 認 rèn *13*
admit defeat 認輸 rèn shū *13*
admit one's mistake 認錯 rèn cuò *13*
adorable 可愛 kě ài *62*
advanced 先進 xiān jìn *84*
after 後 hòu *69*
affection 愛心 ài xīn *62*
after/afterward 以後 yǐ hòu *56*
afterward 後來/然後 hòu lái/rán hòu *69*
afternoon nap 午覺 wǔ jiào *64*
against 反對 fǎn duì *50*
age 歲數 suì shu *10*
agree/accept 同意 tóng yì *73*
Ah! 哎呀!/呀! aī yā/yā *87*
air 空氣 kōng qì *76*
alike 一樣/同樣 yī yàng/tóng yàng *12*
all 所有 suǒ yǒu *55*
all along 從來 cóng lái *85*
all directions 四方 sì fāng *106*
all over the body 週身 zhōu shēn *31*
all right 還可以 hái kě yǐ *16*; 還好 hài hǎo *25*
all year round 常年 cháng nián *37*
allow 給 gěi *98*
already know 已知 yǐ zhī *79*
amount 分量 fèn liàng *19*
and 以及 yǐ jí *56*
...and so on 等等 děng děng *28*
and then 後來/然後 hòu lái/rán hòu *69*; 就 jiù *101*
angry 氣/生氣 qì/shēng qì *83*

anniversary 週年 zhōu nián *31*
answer 回答 huí dá *53*
apologize 道歉 dào qiàn *80*
appear 出現 chū xiàn *15*; 來 lái *85*
appear to be 看來 kàn lái *85*
appearance 樣/樣子 yàng/yàng zi *12*
appetite 胃口 wèi kǒu *94*
applaud 喝彩 hè cǎi *96*
appointment 約會 yuē huì *47*
appropriate 方便 fāng biàn *107*
approve 認同/認可 rèn tóng/rèn kě *13*
archeology 考古學 kǎo gǔ xué *104*
arrive 到 dào *66*; 來到 lái dào *85*
arrived 到了 dào le *66*
around 週/週圍/四週 zhōu/zhōu wéi/sì zhōu *31*
as a result 因而 yīn ér *21*
as well as 以及 yǐ jí *56*
assistant 幫手 bāng shǒu *108*; 助手/助理 zhù shǒu/zhù lǐ *109*
ask/inquire 打聽 dǎ tīng *44*
ask for 要 yào *78*
assemble 會合 huì hé *47*
at ease 放心 fàng xīn *71*
at first 本來 běn lái *85*
at last 最後 zuì hòu *69*
at present 現在 xiàn zài *15*
at the end 末了 mò liǎo *32*
audience 聽眾 tīng zhòng *44*
author 作家/作者 zuò jiā/zuò zhě *68*
auxiliary word 助詞 zhù cí *109*

B

babysit 看孩子 kān hái zi *35*
back 後/後面/後邊 hòu/hòu miàn/hòu bian *69*
back door 後門 hòu mén *69*
ball 球 qiú *34*
ball (dance) 舞會 wǔ huì *49*
ball-shaped object 球 qiú *34*
ballet 芭蕾舞 bā lěi wǔ *49*
balloon 氣球 qì qiú *83*
band 樂隊 yuè duì *46*
bar top 吧臺 bā tái *43*
basketball 藍球 lán qiú *34*
bathroom 廁所 cè suǒ *55*
battery 電池 diàn chí *39*
be a guest 作客 zuò kè *68*
beat 跳 tiào *48*

film/movie 電影 diàn yǐng *39*

finally 最後 zùi hòu *69*

find/found 找到 zhǎo dào *65*

Fine! 好吧 hǎo ba *43*

first birthday 週歲 zhōu sùi *10*

five minutes (time) 五分/五分鐘 wǔ fēn/wǔ fēn zhōng *19*

five points/marks 五分 wǔ fēn *19*

fizzy drink 汽水 qì shuǐ *100*

flavor 味道 wèi dào *80*

flirt 玩弄 wán nòng *61*

float 漂/漂浮 piāo/piāo fú *92*

(to) flower 開花/開放 kāi huā/kāi fàng *72*

fond of 喜/喜歡/喜愛 xǐ/xǐ huān/xǐ ài *26*

football 足球 zú qiú *34*

for 為/為了 wéi/wèi le *22*; 給 gěi *98*

for a long time 久/長久 jiǔ/cháng jiǔ *30*

for a very long time 久久 jiǔ jiǔ *30*

forever 永久 yǒng jiǔ *30*

forgotten 給忘了 gěi wàng le *98*

found out 找出 zhǎo chū *65*

four gang of people 四幫人 sì bāng rén *108*

free 空/有空 kòng/yǒu kòng *76*

frequently 常常/時常 cháng cháng/shí cháng *37*

from now on 今後 jīn hòu *69*

fruit 水果 shuǐ guǒ *100*

fun 好玩 hǎo wán *61*

funny 可笑 kě xiào *16*

furthermore 還有 hái yǒu *25*

G

gas 氣 qì *83*

general knowledge 常識 cháng shí *14*

generous 大方 dà fang *106*

genius 天才 tiān cái *52*

get 得到 dé dào *66*

get hold of 拿到 ná dào *66*

get inside 進去/進入 jìn qù/jìn rù *84*

get involved 介入 jiè rù *88*

get lost 走開 zǒu kāi *72*

get out (of bed) 起牀 qǐ chuáng *103*

get rid of/remove 去 qù *54*

get up 起來 qǐ lái *85*

give 給/給以 gěi/gěi yǐ *98*

give as a present 送給 sòng gěi *98*

glorious 高大 gāo dà *90*

glow 發亮 fā liàng *93*

go for a movie 看電影 kàn diàn yǐng *35*

go 到 dào *66*

go back 回去 huí qù *54*

go in 進去/進入 jìn qù/jìn rù *84*

go out 出去 chū qù *54*

go to 去 qù *54*

go to bed 睡覺 shuì jiào *64*; 上牀 shàng chuáng *103*

grade/rank 等 děng *28*

grandmother (maternal) 外婆 wài pó *58*

guess 猜想 cāi xiǎng *60*

guest 客/客人 kè/kè rén *82*

guest room 客房 kè fáng *82*

H

had a good sleep 睡飽 shuì bǎo *63*

had better 還是 hái shi *25*

half 半 bàn *18*

half day 半天 bàn tiān *18*

half past nine 九點半 jiǔ diǎn bàn *18*

happen 起 qǐ *102*

happily 興衝衝 xīng chōng chōng *91*

happy 喜 xǐ *26*; 歡 huān *27*; 樂 lè *46*; 快樂/愉快 kuài lè/yú kuài *70*

happy 歡喜 huān xǐ *27*; 歡樂 huān lè *27, 46*; 開心 kāi xīn *72*; 興/高興 xìng/gāo xìng *91*

happy event 喜事 xǐ shì *26*

hastily 急忙 jí máng *24*

have a look 看看 kàn kan *35*

have to 祇好/祇得 zhǐ hǎo/zhǐ dé *59*

hear 聽 tīng *44*

heard 聽見/聽到 tīng jiàn/tīng dào *44*

heart palpitation/heartbeat 心跳 xīn tiào *48*

heartening 可喜 kě xǐ *26*

height 高矮/高低 gāo ǎi/gāo dī *90*

(to) help 幫 bāng *108*

(to) help/help 幫忙 bāng máng *24, 108*; 幫助 bāng zhù *108, 109*; 助 zhù *109*

high 高 gāo *90*

high class 上等 shàng děng *28*

high jump 跳高 tiào gāo *48*

high level 高等 gāo děng *90*

highland 高地 gāo dì *90*

hobby 愛好 ài hào *62*

hold a meeting 開會 kāi huì *47*

homework 作業 zuò yè *68*

hour (time) 鐘頭 zhōng tóu *20*

how(?) 怎/怎麼(?) zěn/zěn me *11*

how about it(?) 怎樣(?)/怎麼樣(?) zěn yàng/zěn me yàng *11*

how old(?) 幾歲(?) jǐ sùi *10*

huge 高大 gāo dà *90*

R

raindrops 雨點 yǔ diǎn *17*
rank/grade 等 děng *28*
read (reading materials) 看 kàn *35*
ready to 樂意 lè yì *46*
readymade 現成 xiàn chéng *15*
realize 發覺 fā jué *64*
really/truly 可是 kě shì *16*
reason 因/原因 yīn/yuán yīn *21*; 為什麼(?) wèi shén me *22*
reasoning 道理 dào li *80*
recall 想起 xiǎng qǐ *60*
reckon 想 xiǎng *60*
recognize 認/認得 rèn/rèn de *13*; 識/認識 shí/rèn shi *14*
recollect 回想 huí xiǎng *53*
record/phonograph 唱片 chàng piàn *41*
recover 拿回 ná huí *53*
refer to 説到 shuō dào *66*
refreshments 茶點 chá diǎn *97*
refrigerator 電冰箱 diàn bīng xiāng *39*
regard as 當作 dāng zuò *68*
regular 正常 zhèng cháng *37*
regular customer 常客 cháng kè *82*
relatives of one's mother 外 wài *58*
release 放/放開 fàng/fàng kāi *71*
relieve/help 救助 jiù zhù *109*
relieve oneself 方便 fāng biàn *107*
remember 想起 xiǎng qǐ *60*
remove 去 qù *54*
request 要求 yāo qiú *78*
residence 住所 zhù suǒ *55*
resit a test/exam 補考 bǔ kǎo *104*
return 回 huí *53*
return/give back 還 huán *25*
return/go back 回去 huí qù *54*
return a call (reply) 回電 huí diàn *39*
return book(s) 還書 huán shū *25*
return change (money) 找/找錢 zhǎo/zhǎo qián *65*
return home 回家 huí jiā *53*
return to 回到 huí dào *66*
ride 坐 zuò *86*
ringing (of bells) 鐘聲 zhōng shēng *20*
rinse 漂 piǎo *92*
rise 起來 qǐ lái *85, 102*; 起/起身 qǐ/qǐ shēn *102*
road 道/道路 dào/dào lù *80*

S

salary 薪水 xīn shuǐ *100*

same age 同歲 tóng suì *10*
sample book 樣本 yàng běn *12*
say goodbye 分手 fēn shǒu *19*
scene (of happenings) 現場 xiàn chǎng *15*
school bag 書包 shū bāo *36*
search 找尋 zhǎo xún *65*
seat 坐位 zuò wèi *86*
see 看/看見 kàn/kàn jiàn *35*; 視 shì *40*
see a patient 看病 kàn bìng *35*
see as 視為 shì wéi *40*
see ... off 歡送 huān sòng *27*
sell to 賣給 mài gěi *98*
send (a signal/message) 打 dǎ *33*
senior 太 tài *29*; 高 gāo *90*
sentence-ending particle 呀 ya *87*
separate 分開 fēn kāi *72*
set fire 放火 fàng huǒ *71*
set free 放開 fàng kāi *71*
share work 分工 fēn gōng *19*
shiny 明亮 míng liàng *93*
shout 喝 hè *96*
show 亮 liàng *93*
show improvement 進步 jìn bù *84*
sing 唱/唱歌/歌唱 chàng/chàng gē/gē chàng *41*
sing an opera 唱戲 chàng xì *41*
sing for a living 賣唱 mài chàng *41*
sing in chorus 合唱 hé chàng *41*
sing loudly 高唱 gāo chàng *41*
singer (vocalist) 歌手 gē shǒu *42*
single bed 單人牀 dān rén chuáng *103*
sit 坐 zuò *86*
sit down 坐下 zuò xià *86*
sit in silence 靜坐 jìng zuò *86*
sketch from nature 寫生 xiě shēng *38*
skip a grade/level 跳班 tiào bān *48*
sky 空/天空 kōng/tiān kōng *76*
skydive 跳傘 tiào sǎn *48*
sleep 睡 shuì *63*; 覺/睡覺 jiào/shuì jiào *64*
small token 小意思 xiǎo yì si *74*
smell 氣味 qì wèi *83*
snack 點心 diǎn xīn *17*
so/therefore 因此 yīn cǐ *20*
so long as 祇要 zhǐ yào *59*
so that 以便 yǐ biàn *107*
song 歌 gē *42*
song and dance 歌舞 gē wǔ *49*
soon 不久 bù jiǔ *30*; 快要/快了 kuài yào/kuài le *70*
sorry 對不起 duì bu qǐ *50, 102*
sound 音/聲音 yīn/shēng yīn *45*

List of Radicals

— 1 stroke —

1	一	one
2	丨	down
3	丶	dot
4	丿	left
5	乙	twist
6	亅	hook

— 2 strokes —

7	二	two
8	亠	lid
9	人	man
10	儿	legs
11	入	enter
12	八	eight
13	冂	borders
14	冖	crown
15	冫	ice
16	几	table
17	凵	bowl
18	刀	knife
19	力	strength
20	勹	wrap
21	匕	ladle
22	匚	basket
23	匸	box
24	十	ten
25	卜	divine
26	卩	seal
27	厂	slope
28	厶	cocoon
29	又	right hand

— 3 strokes —

30	口	mouth
31	囗	surround
32	土	earth
33	士	knight
34	夂	follow
35	夊	slow
36	夕	dusk
37	大	big
38	女	woman
39	子	child
40	宀	roof
41	寸	thumb
42	小	small
43	尢	lame
44	尸	corpse
45	屮	sprout
46	山	mountain
47	川	river
48	工	work
49	己	self
50	巾	cloth
51	干	shield
52	幺	coil
53	广	lean-to
54	廴	march
55	廾	clasp
56	弋	dart
57	弓	bow
58	彐	pig's head
59	彡	streaks
60	彳	step

— 4 strokes —

61	心	heart
62	戈	lance
63	戶	door
64	手	hand
65	支	branch
66	攴	knock
67	文	pattern
68	斗	peck
69	斤	axe
70	方	square
71	无	lack
72	日	sun
73	曰	say
74	月	moon
75	木	tree
76	欠	yawn
77	止	toe
78	歹	chip
79	殳	club
80	毋	don't
81	比	compare
82	毛	fur
83	氏	clan
84	气	breath
85	水	water
86	火	fire
87	爪	claws
88	父	father
89	爻	crisscross
90	爿	bed
91	片	slice
92	牙	tooth
93	牛	cow
94	犬	dog

— 5 strokes —

95	玄	dark
96	玉	jade
97	瓜	melon
98	瓦	tile
99	甘	sweet
100	生	birth
101	用	use
102	田	field
103	疋	bolt
104	疒	sick
105	癶	back
106	白	white
107	皮	skin
108	皿	dish
109	目	eye
110	矛	spear
111	矢	arrow
112	石	rock
113	示	sign
114	禸	track
115	禾	grain

— 6 strokes —

116	穴	cave
117	立	stand
118	竹	bamboo
119	米	rice
120	糸	silk
121	缶	crock
122	网	net
123	羊	sheep
124	羽	wings
125	老	old
126	而	beard
127	耒	plow
128	耳	ear
129	聿	brush
130	肉	meat
131	臣	bureaucrat
132	自	small nose
133	至	reach
134	臼	mortar
135	舌	tongue
136	舛	discord
137	舟	boat
138	艮	stubborn
139	色	color
140	艸	grass
141	虍	tiger
142	虫	bug
143	血	blood
144	行	go
145	衣	gown
146	襾	cover

— 7 strokes —

147	見	see
148	角	horn
149	言	words
150	谷	valley
151	豆	flask
152	豕	pig
153	豸	snake
154	貝	cowrie
155	赤	red
156	走	walk
157	足	foot
158	身	torso
159	車	car
160	辛	bitter
161	辰	early
162	辵	halt
163	邑	city
164	酉	wine
165	釆	sift
166	里	village

— 8 strokes —

167	金	gold
168	長	long
169	門	gate
170	阜	mound
171	隶	grab
172	隹	dove
173	雨	rain
174	青	green
175	非	wrong

— 9 strokes —

176	面	face
177	革	hide
178	韋	walk off
179	韭	leeks
180	音	tone
181	頁	head
182	風	wind
183	飛	fly
184	食	food
185	首	chief
186	香	scent

— 10 strokes —

187	馬	horse
188	骨	bone
189	高	tall
190	髟	hair
191	鬥	fight
192	鬯	mixed wine
193	鬲	cauldron
194	鬼	ghost

— 11 strokes —

195	魚	fish
196	鳥	bird
197	鹵	salt
198	鹿	deer
199	麥	wheat
200	麻	hemp

— 12 strokes —

201	黃	yellow
202	黍	millet
203	黑	black
204	黹	embroider

— 13 strokes —

205	黽	toad
206	鼎	tripod
207	鼓	drum
208	鼠	mouse

— 14 strokes —

209	鼻	big nose
210	齊	line-up

— 15 strokes —

211	齒	teeth

— 16 strokes —

212	龍	dragon
213	龜	tortoise

— 17 strokes —

214	龠	flute